M000274532

Making Books with Pockets

The series of monthly activity books you've been waiting for!

Enliven every month of the year with fun, exciting learning projects that students can proudly present in a unique book format.

Each month has lessons for art, writing, reading, math, science, social studies, and poetry.

Contents

Michelle Barnett, Caitlin Rabanera, and **Ann Switzer** have taught first, second, and third grade. Their teaching experiences have involved working with limited-English-speaking students from many parts of the world, supervising student teachers, and conducting inservice sessions for colleagues. They are currently teaching in Southern California.

Congratulations on your purchase of some of the finest teaching materials in the world.

For information about other Evan-Moor products, call 1-800-777-4362 or FAX 1-800-777-4332

Visit our website http://www.evan-moor.com. Check the Product Updates link for supplements, additions, and corrections for this book.

Authors: Michelle Barnett
            Caitlin Rabanera
            Ann Switzer
Editors: Marilyn Evans
            Jill Norris
Copy Editor: Cathy Harber
Illustrator: Jo Larsen
Designer: Cheryl Puckett
Desktop: Shannon Frederickson

Evan-Moor
EDUCATIONAL PUBLISHERS
EMC 588

May's Special Days

Here are ideas for celebrating some of the other special days in May.

May 1 _____ **May Day**
Have each student draw his or her favorite flower (or make a tissue paper flower) and secretly give it to a friend.

May 5 _____ **Leo Lionni's Birthday**
Read a Leo Lionni book such as *Swimmy* or *It's Mine* to your class.

First Week in May _____ **National Postcard Week**
Have each student write a postcard. Why not write to Leo Lionni and tell him what you liked in one of his books. Send the postcards to Mr. Lionni in care of his publisher: Pantheon, a Division of Random House, 201 E. 50th St., New York, NY 10022.

Second Week in May _____ **National Pickle Week**
Bring in several kinds of sweet pickles and dill pickles. Have a taste test. Graph the results.

May 22 _____ **Arnold Lobel's Birthday**
Read a "Frog and Toad" book. Have students write a summary of their favorite chapter.

May 30 _____ **One-Foot Day**
On this date in 1975, Don Carter set the world's record for balancing on one foot—8 hours and 46 minutes. See how long you can balance on one foot.

National Salad Month
Try some unusual ways to eat your veggies. Make a different kind of salad in class each week. (Page 81 features a nasturtium salad!)

May

Sunday	Monday	Tuesday	Wednesday	Thursday	Friday	Saturday

3

How to Make Pocket Books

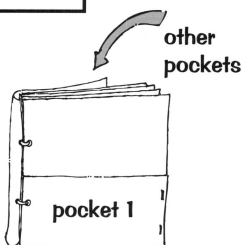

other pockets

pocket 1

Each pocket book has a cover and three or more pockets. Choose construction paper colors that are appropriate to the theme of the book. Using several colors in a book creates an effective presentation.

Materials

- 12" x 18" (30.5 x 45.5 cm) piece of construction paper for each pocket
- cover as described for each book
- hole punch
- stapler
- string, ribbon, twine, raffia, etc., for ties

Steps to Follow

1. Fold the construction paper to create a pocket. After folding, the paper should measure 12" (30.5 cm) square.

2. Staple the right side of each pocket closed.

3. Punch two or three holes in the left side of each pocket and the cover.

4. Fasten the book together using your choice of material as ties.

5. Glue the poem or information strips onto each pocket as shown on the overview pages of each book.

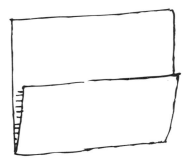

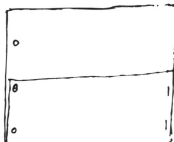

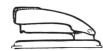

CINCO DE MAYO

Celebrate Cinco de Mayo by making a book built around a poem that tells about the holiday. Students will experience art, oral and written language, and math activities all organized and displayed in this festive pocket book.

Cinco de Mayo

This poem can also be used for pocket chart activities throughout the month:
  • Chant the poem
  • Listen for rhyming words
  • Learn new vocabulary
  • Identify sight words
  • Put words or lines in the correct order

Use the picture dictionary to introduce new vocabulary and as a spelling reference. Students can add new pictures, labels, and descriptive adjectives to the page as their vocabulary increases.

Use this form for story writing or as a place to record additional vocabulary words.

BIBLIOGRAPHY

Fiesta by Beatriz McConnie Zapater; Simon & Schuster, 1992.
Fiesta Cinco de Mayo by June Behrens; Golden Gate Junior Book, 1978.
Too Many Tamales by Gary Soto; Putnam & Grosset Group, 1993.

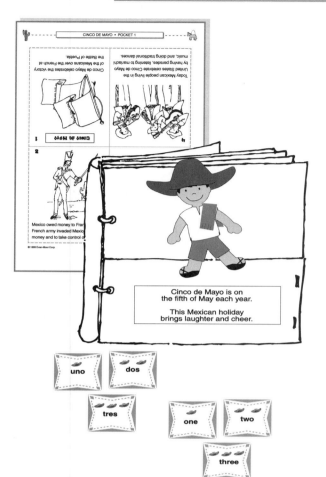

POCKET 1

Mexican Paper Doll   **pages 9–11**
Students cut and paste to make a paper doll wearing colorful traditional clothing as might be seen on Cinco de Mayo.

**Two Games to Learn
Spanish and
English Vocabulary**   **pages 12–15**
Using the word cards provided, students play two games that will help them learn Spanish and English word meanings.

Cinco de Mayo Minibook   **page 16**
Just two folds are all it takes to create a little book that tells a bit about the history of Cinco de Mayo. Students can color the pictures to make their books extra interesting.

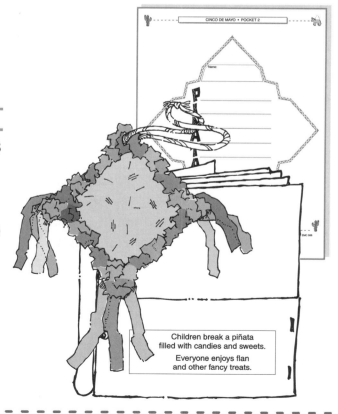

POCKET 2

Make a Piñata   **pages 17 and 18**
Create a traditional star-shaped piñata from construction paper and tissue paper. Stuff it with newspaper for a 3-D look.

Piñata Acrostic Verse   **pages 19 and 20**
Students learn about acrostic verse by reading and discussing the several models provided. Then they write their own piñata acrostic verse on a piñata writing form.

POCKET 3

Make a Mexican Flag   pages 21 and 22
Read the information provided about the symbols on the Mexican flag. Then students make their own Mexican flags.

The Mexican Flag   page 23
Students write about the Mexican flag using this writing form.

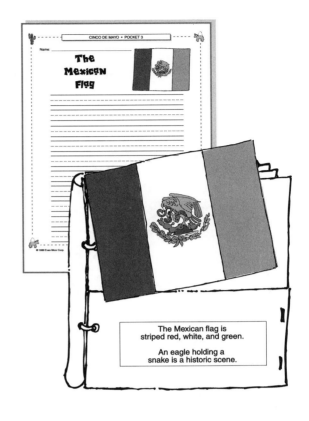

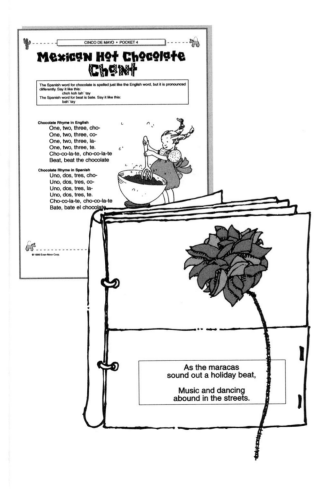

POCKET 4

Celebrate with a Classroom Fiesta   page 24
Follow a recipe to make yummy Mexican Hot Chocolate. Make cascarones—eggs filled with confetti—to crack over a friend's head!

Mexican Hot Chocolate Chant   page 25
Mexican children say this chant as they stir the chocolate.

Tissue Paper Flowers   page 26
These easy-to-make flowers are a Mexican tradition. They'll really give a festive look to your classroom.

Materials

- construction paper
  white, 12" (30.5 cm) square
  red, 6" (15 cm) square
  green, 6" (15 cm) square
- black marker
- scissors
- glue

Steps 1 and 2

Steps to Follow

1. Tear the red and green squares across the diagonal to make a triangular shape. Tear in a slightly bulging curve. You will use the larger of the two pieces of the squares.

2. Glue the red triangle to the top left corner of the white construction paper. Glue the green triangle to the bottom right corner.

3. Use a black marker to write "Cinco de Mayo" in the center of the page from corner to corner.

Step 3

Mexican Paper Doll

Dress this paper doll in traditional holiday costume.

Materials

- doll pattern on page 10, reproduced on manila construction paper
- tagboard templates of clothing, made from patterns on page 11
- construction paper
  sarape—red, 4" (10 cm) square
  shirt—white, 4" (10 cm) square
  sombrero and pants—brown, 6" (15 cm) square
- scraps of black, white, green, and yellow
- scissors
- glue

Steps to Follow

1. Cut out the paper doll body.

2. Trace the sombrero and pants onto the brown paper and cut them out.

3. Trace the shirt onto white paper and cut it out.

4. Trace the sarape onto red paper and cut it out.

5. Glue the clothing onto the paper doll, placing the sarape on top of the shirt.

6. Tear or cut out hair from black scraps. Glue hair to top and sides of head.

7. Tear tiny strips of black paper to make sandals. Glue one piece to bottom of foot. Glue two other pieces at a diagonal to create straps.

8. Cut a slit in the sombrero as shown. Slip the doll's head into the slit so that the sombrero sits down over the head. Attach it with glue.

9. Use scraps of green and yellow to decorate the sombrero and the sarape.

10. Fringe the edge of the sarape.

**Mexican Paper Doll
Body Pattern**

10

Mexican Paper Doll Clothing Patterns

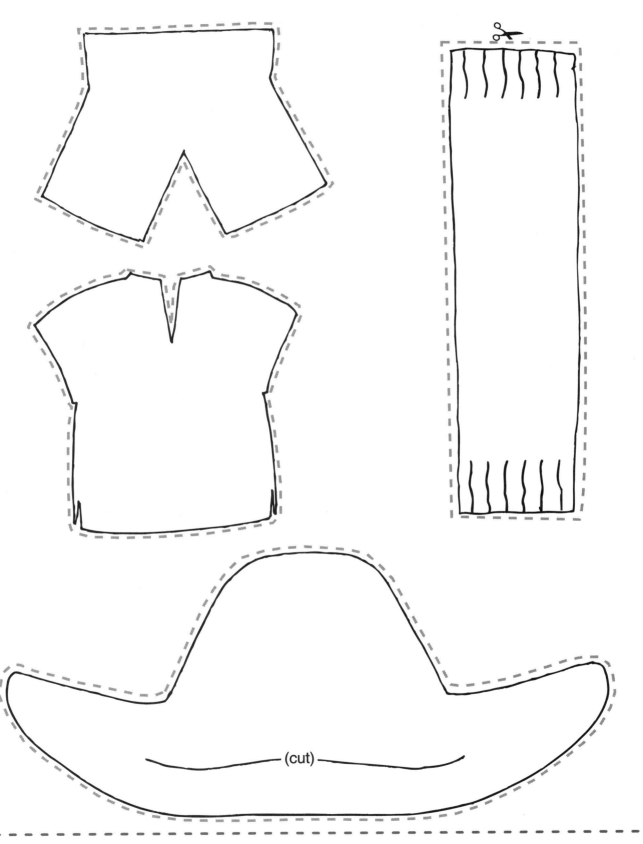

(cut)

Two Games to Learn Spanish and English Vocabulary

Reproduce the word cards on pages 13–15 and use them in the following games to help students learn English and Spanish meanings. Make additional word cards when your class is proficient with those provided.

Reproduce a copy of the word cards for students to add to this pocket of their Cinco de Mayo books. Cut them apart and put them in an envelope.

 Pairs Match

In this concentration game for 2–6 players, students match English and Spanish words with the same meaning.

1. Use as many pairs of word cards as you think your students can comfortably work.

2. Mix up the cards and lay them facedown in rows.

3. Have the players take turns flipping over two cards at a time and reading the words.

4. If the words have the same meaning in both Spanish and English, the student keeps the pair and takes another turn. For example, May and Mayo.

5. If the words do not have the same meaning, the student flips the cards back over and the next student takes a turn.

6. After all of the pairs have been matched, the winner is the student with the most pairs of word cards.

 Partner Match-Up

Students read and listen to words in English and Spanish until they find the student whose word matches their own.

1. Use pairs of Spanish and English word cards—enough for each child in the class to have one card. If you do not have an even number of students, you may need to join in the play.

2. Pass out a card to each student.

3. Students stroll around the room reading their cards to each student they meet.

4. When they find the classmate with the matching card in the other language, the students sit down together. Play until all students are seated.

5. Collect, shuffle, and redistribute cards. Repeat the activity.

Note: When the game begins, do not allow students to race around to find their partners. The purpose of this activity is to read and listen to different words.

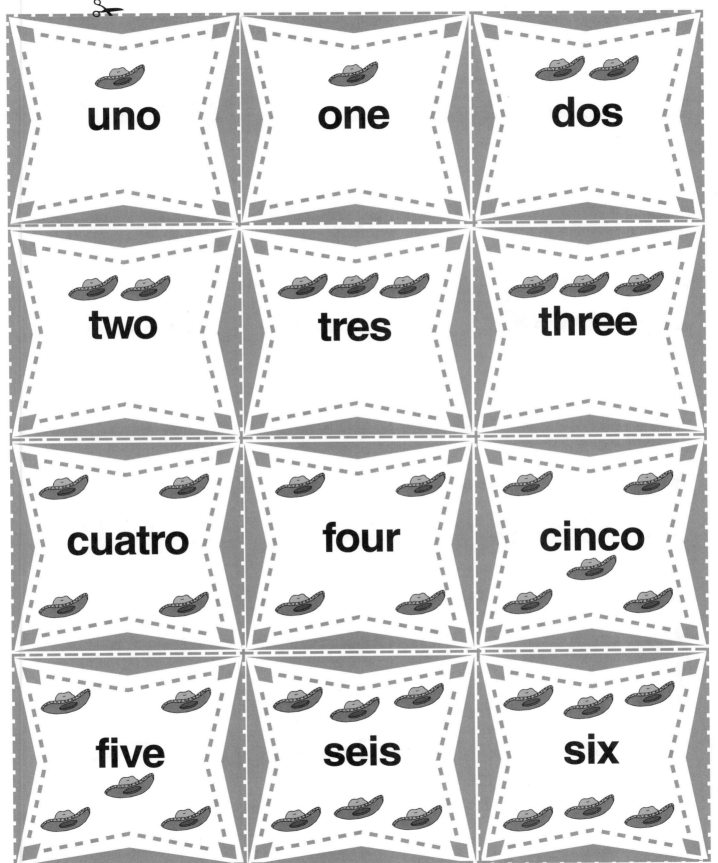

uno

one

dos

two

tres

three

cuatro

four

cinco

five

seis

six

13

mayo

 May

 septiembre

 September

 enero

 January

 sombrero

 hat

 libro

 book

 zapata

 shoe

adiós	**good-bye**	**mañana**
morning	**buenas días**	**good day**
gracias	**thank you**	**¿Cómo esta usted?**
How are you?	**bueno**	**good**

Making Books with Pockets • May • EMC 588

Cinco de Mayo celebrates the victory of the Mexicans over the French at the Battle of Puebla.

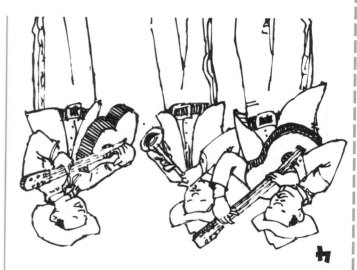

Cinco de Mayo

1

Today Mexican people living in the United States celebrate Cinco de Mayo by having parades, listening to mariachi music, and doing traditional dances.

4

2

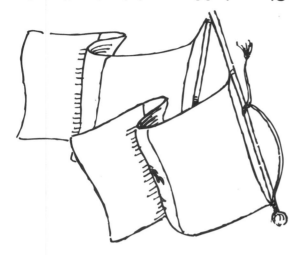

Mexico owed money to France. The French army invaded Mexico to get the money and to take control of the land.

3

Mexico's small army miraculously defeated the French on May 5, 1862, in the town of Puebla.

Materials

- two 12" (30.5 cm) square pieces of construction paper—any color
- tagboard piñata templates, made using the pattern on page 18
- 1" (2.5 cm) squares of tissue paper—any color
- nine 1" x 6" (2.5 x 15 cm) strips of tissue paper—any color
- shredded newspaper
- pencil
- 2' (61 cm) piece of yarn or roving
- crayons
- glue
- hole punch

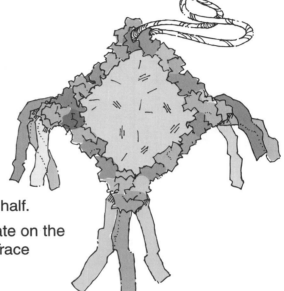

Steps to Follow

1. Fold both pieces of construction paper in half.

2. Lay the straight edge of the piñata template on the fold of each piece of construction paper. Trace around the template and then cut out the piñata shapes.

3. Open the two pieces of construction paper.

4. Add designs to the piñata with crayons.

5. Glue the strips of tissue paper to three adjacent points on one of the pieces of construction paper.

6. Glue the two pieces of the piñata together, leaving an opening for stuffing. (Make sure that the tissue strips attach on the inside.)

7. Use shredded newspaper to stuff the piñata. Glue the opening closed.

8. Wrap each square of tissue paper around the eraser end of a pencil. Holding the tissue paper onto the eraser, dip the tissue into glue. Then press the glued tissue onto the edge of the piñata. Glue tissue pieces around the entire piñata. "Fluff" the tissue paper to make it stand up.

9. Punch a hole in the top of the piñata and insert yarn for hanging.

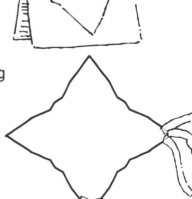

Piñata Template

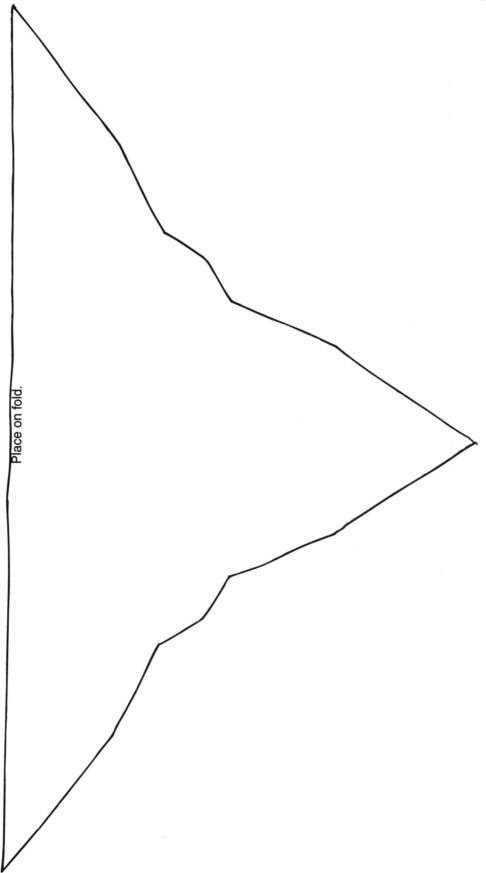

Place on fold.

Piñata Acrostic Verse

An acrostic verse is a composition in which each line begins with a letter of the subject word. The lines of the verse describe the subject of the verse.

> **P**retty decoration filled with treats and surprises hidden
> **I**nside a tissue-covered crock;
> **N**o one wants to be left out
> **A**s the breaking blow is swung
> **T**hrowing goodies to the floor.
> **A**ll the children scramble with glee.

Steps to Follow

1. Explain the acrostic form to your students, using several models that you've written on charts or overhead transparencies.

> **C**hocolate is the best I think.
> **A**nother favorite is caramel.
> **N**ow won't you have some?
> **D**entists say it's not good for you.
> **Y**et, who can resist a bite or two?
>
> **P**eople have fun
> **A**nd they play games.
> **R**ed balloons are everywhere.
> **T**he food is yummy.
> **Y**ou get party favors.

2. Hang up six large pieces of paper and head each with one letter of the word "piñata."

3. Brainstorm with the class and write phrases that relate to a piñata and begin with each letter of the word. You may have to assist by rearranging words or suggesting synonyms or alternate ways of stating an idea so that the phrases begin with the correct letters.

4. Let students write their own acrostic verses on a copy of page 20. They may use phrases from the class lists or make up their own statements.

Name:

P
I
Ñ
A
T
A

Make a Mexican Flag

Before your students make a Mexican flag, share a picture of it. Look for one in library books or a World Almanac. Then tell your students about the symbols on the flag and what they stand for. You will need to discuss some of the vocabulary.

Mexico's colorful flag represents the pride of the Mexican people in their country and in their history. The green band stands for *independence*, white for *religion*, and red represents *unity*. These three ideals were what the Mexican people were fighting for during Mexico's war of independence from Spain.

Centered on the white band is Mexico's coat of arms—a symbol that has ancient origins. One of the native groups that inhabited Mexico before the Spanish arrived was the Aztecs. According to legend, the Aztecs were told to settle and build a city where they found an eagle eating a snake while sitting atop a cactus on an island in the middle of a lake. They found exactly that scene and built their city on the site of what is now Mexico City.

Materials

- pattern on page 22, reproduced for each student
- construction paper
  red, 4" x 9" (10 x 23 cm)
  green, 9" x 12" (23 x 30.5 cm)
- glue
- crayons

Steps to Follow

1. Glue the red construction paper on the right side of the green paper.

2. Glue the eagle pattern to the left of the red paper.

3. Have students color the eagle emblem.

Mexican Flag Pattern

Name: _____

The Mexican Flag

_____
_____
_____
_____
_____
_____
_____
_____
_____
_____
_____
_____
_____
_____
_____
_____
_____
_____
_____
_____
_____
_____

Celebrate with a Classroom Fiesta

After learning all about the festivities of Cinco de Mayo, your students will want to celebrate, too! Plan your fiesta to include breaking a piñata (purchase one at a party supply store), enjoying a treat of Mexican chocolate, and making traditional tissue paper flowers to wear and cascarones to break on your heads.

Put the flower and a copy of the hot chocolate chant in the final pocket of the Cinco de Mayo book.

Mexican Hot Chocolate

Before making the chocolate, learn the traditional chant on page 25 and say it while stirring the chocolate.

Mexicans were the first to make hot chocolate. They drink it all year long despite the hot weather. Traditional Mexican hot chocolate is made using chocolate tablets flavored with cinnamon and orange.

How to make one serving:

1. Mix the following ingredients in a cup:
   1 teaspoon (3 g) cocoa
   2 teaspoons (8 g) sugar
   ¼ cup (40 g) powdered milk
   ½ teaspoon (1 g) cinnamon

2. Fill the cup with hot water and stir.

3. Add a bit of orange rind.

4. Top with whipped cream.

Cascarones

"Cascarones" means eggshells. Empty eggshells are filled with colorful confetti, which is released by cracking the eggs over your friends' heads! Be sure to have your fun where the "mess" can be easily contained and cleaned up.

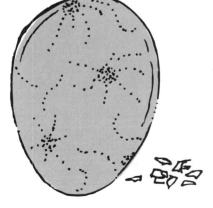

Steps to Follow

1. Remove a small piece of shell from one end of the egg.
   Poke a tiny hole in the other end and blow out the contents.

2. Wash out the eggshells and let them dry.

3. Let students decorate the shells with marking pens and glitter.

4. Fill the eggshells with confetti. (Buy packages at a party supply store.)

5. Glue tissue paper over the holes in the shells.

Mexican Hot Chocolate Chant

The Spanish word for chocolate is spelled just like the English word, but it is pronounced differently. Say it like this:

> choh koh lah´ tay

The Spanish word for beat is bate. Say it like this:

> bah´ tay

Chocolate Rhyme in English

One, two, three, cho-
One, two, three, co-
One, two, three, la-
One, two, three, te.
Cho-co-la-te, cho-co-la-te
Beat, beat the chocolate

Chocolate Rhyme in Spanish

Uno, dos, tres, cho-
Uno, dos, tres, co-
Uno, dos, tres, la-
Uno, dos, tres, te.
Cho-co-la-te, cho-co-la-te
Bate, bate el chocolate

Tissue Paper Flowers

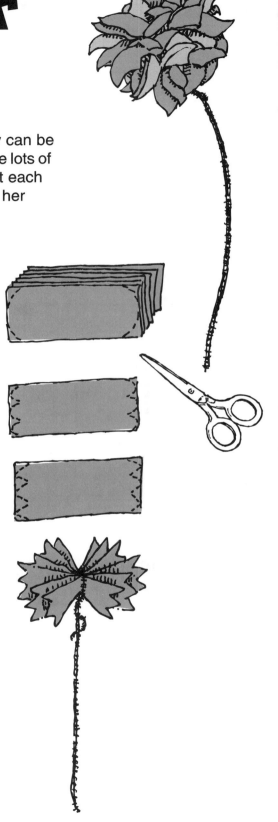

Tissue paper flowers are a Mexican tradition. They can be found in sizes from small to absolutely gigantic. Make lots of these to decorate the classroom for your fiesta. Let each student pick one to adorn the final pocket of his or her Cinco de Mayo book.

Materials

- 6" x 10" (15 x 25.5 cm) pieces of tissue paper in assorted colors
  (Hint: Cut the pack of tissue in half, then open it up and cut 6" lengths.)

- chenille stems

- scissors

Steps to Follow

1. Lay 6 pieces of tissue on top of each other. (Use the same color or mix colors.)

2. Round or scallop the ends or cut them in a zigzag pattern.

3. Gather the tissue paper together in the middle for a "bow tie" effect.

4. Wrap one end of a chenille stem around the gathered tissue and twist it to secure the tissue.

5. Carefully pull each layer apart to make the flower. After a few tries, students will get the idea of "fluffing and scrunching" to make a puffy flower.

Note: Reproduce this page and page 28 to label each of the four pockets of the Cinco do Mayo book.

Cinco de Mayo is on the fifth of May each year.

This Mexican holiday brings laughter and cheer.

Pocket 1

Children break a piñata filled with candies and sweets.

Everyone enjoys flan and other fancy treats.

Pocket 2

The Mexican flag is striped red, white, and green.

An eagle holding a snake is a historic scene.

Pocket 3

As the maracas sound out a holiday beat,

Music and dancing abound in the streets.

Pocket 4

Making Books with Pockets • May • EMC 588

stick

sombrero

señor

candy

piñata

sun

eagle

cactus

snake

maracas

señorita

Making Books with Pockets • May • EMC 588

Name: _____

Cinco de
Mayo

_____
_____
_____
_____
_____
_____
_____
_____
_____
_____
_____
_____
_____
_____
_____
_____
_____
_____
_____
_____
_____
_____
_____
_____

Dinosaurs

Dinosaurs fascinate kids. This pocket book presents activities across the curriculum using this motivating topic. Enhance your science curriculum as you learn about herbivores, carnivores, flying reptiles, and the theories of how dinosaurs became extinct. Students will create their own original writing and practice recording factual information.

Dinosaurs Book

These pages show and tell what is in each pocket.

Step-by-step directions and patterns for the activities that go in each pocket.

Use the picture dictionary to introduce new vocabulary and as a spelling reference. Students can add new pictures, labels, and descriptive adjectives to the page as their vocabulary increases.

Use this form for story writing or as a place to record additional vocabulary words.

BIBLIOGRAPHY

Digging Up Dinosaurs by Aliki; Harper & Row Publishing, 1988.

The Dinosaur Alphabet Book by Jerry Pallotta; Charlesbridge Publishing, 1991.

A Dinosaur Named After Me by Bernard Most; Harcourt Brace & Co., 1991.

Dinosaurs Are Different by Aliki; HarperCollins Publishers, 1985.

The News about Dinosaurs by Patricia Lauber; Aladdin, 1994.

What Happened to the Dinosaurs? by Franklin M. Branley; HarperCollins Publishers, 1989.

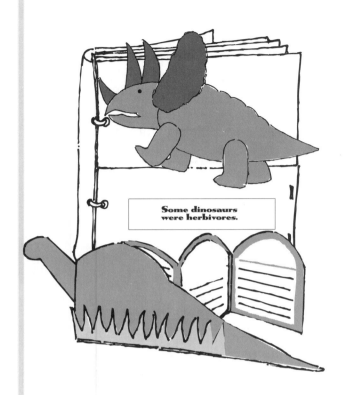

Some dinosaurs were herbivores.

Accordion
Apatosaurus Book   pages 36 and 37

Just add a head and a tail and this simple accordion-folded book becomes an *Apatosaurus*. Writing suggestions are given for completing the book.

Triceratops   pages 38–42

Reproduce information about *Triceratops* for individual students or share it using an overhead transparency. Then transfer what was learned to a simple report form. Cut, paste, and tear to make a charming dinosaur to accompany the report.

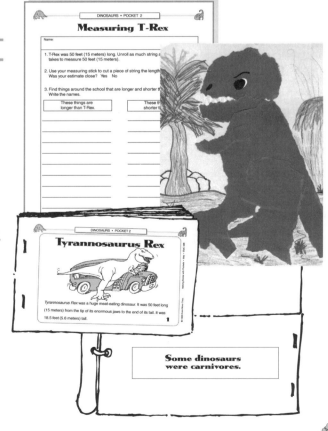

DINOSAURS • POCKET 2

Measuring T-Rex

Name:

1. T-Rex was 50 feet (15 meters) long. Unroll as much string a takes to measure 50 feet (15 meters).

2. Use your measuring stick to cut a piece of string the length Was your estimate close?   Yes   No

3. Find things around the school that are longer and shorter th Write the names.

These things are longer than T-Rex.	These th shorter t

DINOSAURS • POCKET 2

Tyrannosaurus Rex

Tyrannosaurus Rex was a huge meat-eating dinosaur. It was 50 feet long (15 meters) from the tip of its enormous jaws to the end of its tail. It was 18.5 feet (5.6 meters) tall.

Some dinosaurs were carnivores.

Tyrannosaurus
Rex Minibook   pages 43 and 44

Reproduce and compile this minibook so that students can read about the fiercest of all the dinosaurs.

Torn-Paper T-Rex   page 45

Terrible *Tyrannosaurus Rex* stomps across a crayoned background. The torn-paper technique makes him look quite spectacular.

Measuring T-Rex   pages 46 and 47

Students cut a piece of string to show the length of T-Rex and then find items around the school that are longer and shorter than this prehistoric giant.

POCKET 3

A Pteranodon Report   **pages 48–51**

After reading and hearing information about this flying reptile, students write about *Pteranodon* and bind their reports into individual books with the illustrated cover and skeleton drawing provided.

Some prehistoric reptiles could fly.

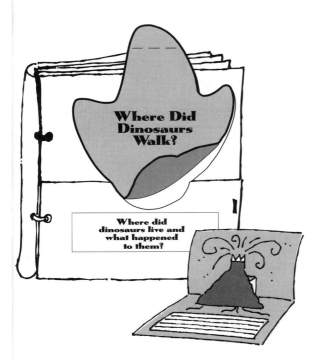

Where Did Dinosaurs Walk?

Where did dinosaurs live and what happened to them?

POCKET 4

Where Did Dinosaurs Walk?   **pages 52–55**

In making this shape book, students will discover that dinosaurs lived all over the world.

How Did Dinosaurs Become Extinct?   **pages 56–60**

This pop-up book illustrates two theories about what caused dinosaurs to disappear.

POCKET 5

If I Were a Dinosaur   **pages 61–63**

Following the format used by Bernard Most in *A Dinosaur Named After Me*, students make up their own dinosaur names and then complete a poem to tell what they would be like as a dinosaur.

The background for this pocket book cover is made using torn paper. If your students have not had practice with the torn-paper technique, practice with scrap paper before beginning the project.

Materials

- 12" (30.5 cm) square of light brown construction paper
- scraps of light and dark green, brown, and blue construction paper
- dinosaur clip art on page 35
- black marking pen
- scissors
- glue

Steps to Follow

1. Tear strips of dark brown paper for tree trunks.

2. Use light and dark green paper to tear 4 or 5 palmlike leaves per tree.

3. Tear dark green paper to make land. Overlap pieces to give a sense of perspective.

4. Tear a blue lake.

5. Glue all the pieces onto the brown paper to create a pleasing scene.

6. Color and cut out the dinosaur patterns and glue them onto the background. (Another option would be to use Ellison® machine cutouts.)

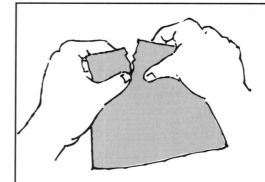

Instruct students to hold the paper between the thumb and forefinger of one hand and to tear with the same fingers of the other hand. As you tear, move the holding fingers along so that they guide the tearing fingers. Practice tearing circles, ovals, "straight," and curved lines.

Dinosaur Clip Art

Making Books with Pockets • May • EMC 588

Accordion Apatosaurus Book

Materials

- 6" x 18" (15 x 45.5 cm) bright green construction paper
- patterns on page 37, reproduced on green construction paper
- 2½" x 8" (6 x 20 cm) light green construction paper
- white and black scraps of construction paper
- 4½" x 6" (11 x 15 cm) writing paper—4 per student
- black marker
- scissors
- glue

Steps to Follow

1. Accordion-fold the bright green construction paper as shown.

2. Round the top of the paper.

3. Cut out the head and tail.

4. Glue the head behind the first fold. Glue the tail on the right side of the front page.

5. Cut the light green construction paper to resemble grass.

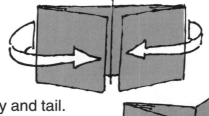

6. Glue the grass to the bottom of *Apatosaurus's* body and tail.

7. Use scraps to make eyes. Draw a mouth using the black marker.

8. Round the top edges of the writing paper and glue them to the inside pages of the dinosaur book.

Writing Ideas

- Read about *Apatosaurus* and write a class poem. Students copy the poem in their individual books.
- Write one fact learned about the *Apatosaurus* on each page.
- Provide story starters and use the accordion book for creative writing.

    The Apatosaurus was about to eat me when…
    When I had an Apatosaurus for a pet, I...
    The most amazing thing about the Apatosaurus is...

Capable writers will need more writing space. Staple additional pages to the last page of the book.

Head and Tail Patterns

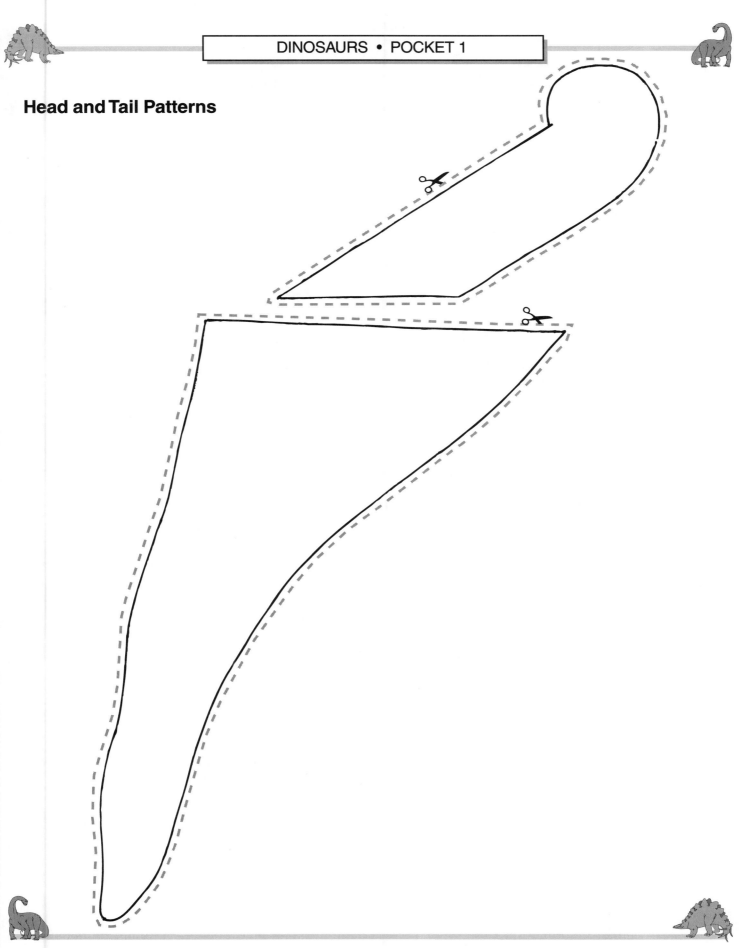

Triceratops

Triceratops was one of the dinosaurs with horns. In fact, its name means "three-horned face."

Triceratops was the largest and the heaviest of the horned dinosaurs. It weighed about 5 tons (4 metric tons) and was over 25 feet (8 meters) long.

Triceratops was a four-legged plant eater. It browsed the plains looking for food. It could snip off tree branches with its sharp turtlelike beak and chop them up with its scissor-sharp teeth.

It had a smooth, solid neck shield and three horns. One was a short, thick nose horn. Two were enormous 40-inch-long (a little over one meter), curved horns pointing forward from above the dinosaur's eyes.

This dinosaur had no real enemies. The horns, neck shield, and tough, leathery skin made it well protected.

Triceratops fossils have been found in the states of Montana and Wyoming in the United States and in Alberta and British Columbia in Canada.

My Triceratops Report

Name:	Date:

The name *Triceratops* means

It was named this because

Triceratops was an ☐ an herbivore ☐ a carnivore

This means that *Triceratops* ate

I know other facts about *Triceratops*:	Here is where *Triceratops* lived in North America.
1.	
2.	British Columbia Alberta Montana Wyoming
3.	

Cut-and-Paste
Triceratops

Materials

- page 41 and 42, reproduced on light brown construction paper
- 5" (13 cm) square of dark brown construction paper
- scraps of black and dark brown construction paper
- glue
- scissors

Steps to Follow

1. Cut out the *Triceratops'* head, body, and legs.

2. Glue the head and the legs to the body. Glue two legs on the front half of the body and two on the back half, angling them so that the dinosaur appears to be walking.

3. Tear a crescent-shaped neck shield from dark brown construction paper. Glue it between the body and the head.

4. Cut three horns from scraps of dark brown paper and glue them to the head.

5. Cut one eye using black scraps and glue it to the *Triceratops'* head.

Triceratops Body Pattern

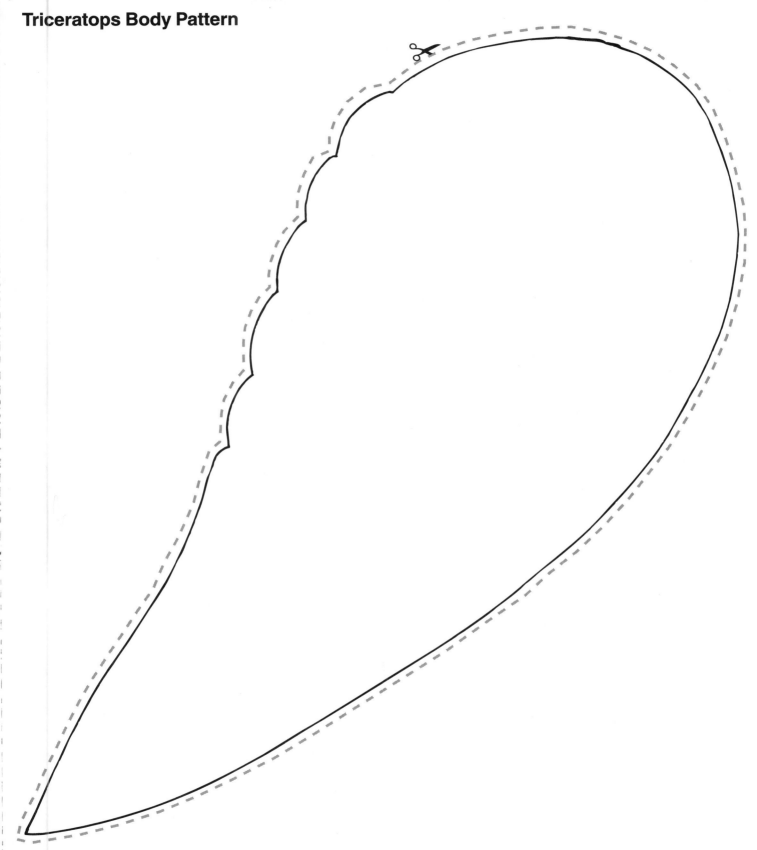

Triceratops Head and Leg Patterns

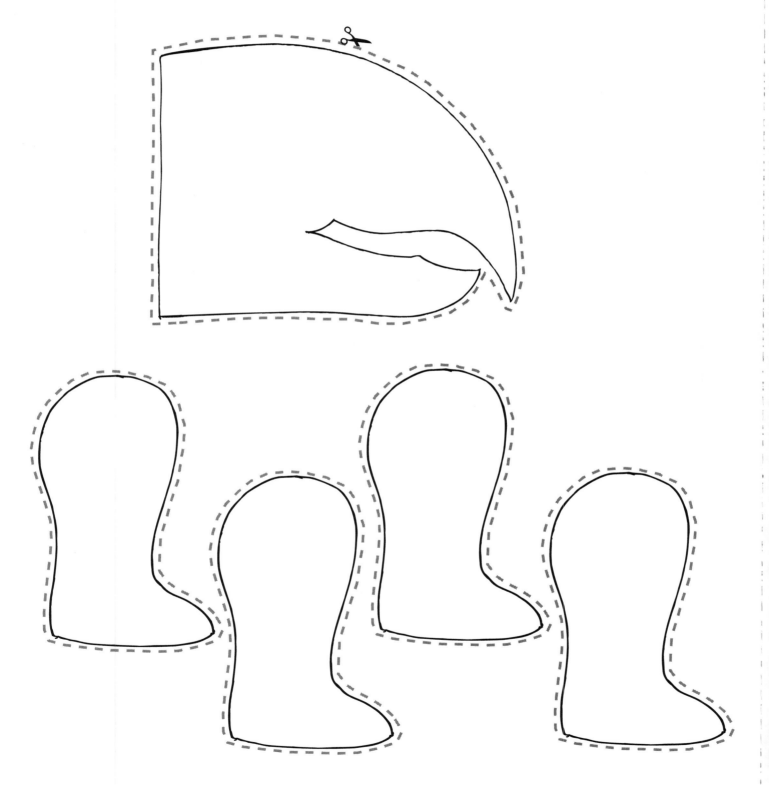

Tyrannosaurus Rex

Tyrannosaurus Rex was a huge meat-eating dinosaur. It was 50 feet long (15 meters) from the tip of its enormous jaws to the end of its tail. It was 18.5 feet (5.6 meters) tall.

1

Tyrannosaurus Rex was a fierce predator. Its jaws were lined with six-inch-long (15 centimeters), razor-sharp teeth. Not only that, it had 8-inch-long (20 centimeters) claws on its feet.

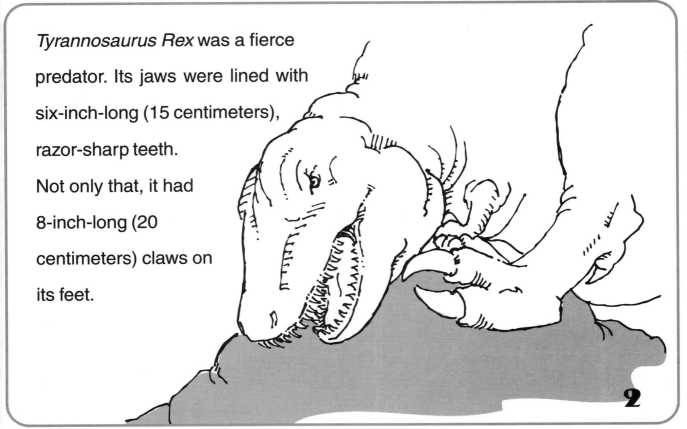

2

Making Books with Pockets • May • EMC 588

Tyrannosaurus Rex had long, strong hind legs, but its arms were very short—less than a yard (meter) long. Scientists don't know what these short arms were used for. Perhaps they helped T-Rex get up from a lying-down position.

3

Making Books with Pockets • May • EMC 588

© 1999 Evan-Moor Corp.

Tyrannosaurus Rex was not very fast moving. It stalked young duckbills and other easy-to-catch prey. It used its powerful jaws and sharp talons to capture and kill its prey.

4

Making Books with Pockets • May • EMC 588

© 1999 Evan-Moor Corp.

Torn-Paper T-Rex

Materials

- 9" x 12" (23 x 30.5 cm) manila drawing paper
- brown construction paper
  head—4 ½" x 5" (11 x 13 cm)
  body—5" x 6" (13 x 15 cm)
  hind legs—two 4" x 6" (10 x 15 cm)
  tail—2" x 5" (5 x 13 cm)
  arm—1" x 3" (2.5 x 7.5 cm)
- scraps of black and white construction paper
- glue
- crayons
- marking pens

Steps to Follow

1. Color a background on the manila paper to represent the habitat of a *Tyrannosaurus Rex*—trees, a volcano, etc.

2. Tear the head piece into an oval. Tear a slit in the lower half of the oval to make the mouth. Use scraps of black and white to make the eye, teeth, and nostril.

3. Tear the body piece into an oval. Glue the body to the head, slanting it slightly.

4. Tear both leg pieces into strong hind legs with three toes each.

5. Glue one leg to the body toward the back and the other leg toward the front.

6. Tear a tail and glue it behind the body.

7. Tear one arm and glue it onto the upper body.

8. Glue T-Rex to the background.

Measuring T-Rex

Young students have not yet developed a frame of reference to help them visualize the size of things when merely told the dimensions. They'll have a graphic understanding of the immensity of *Tyrannosaurus Rex* when they complete this activity.

Materials

- record form on page 47, reproduced for each student
- ball of string for each group
- yardstick or meterstick for each group
- one pair of scissors for each group
- pencils

Steps to Follow

1. If your students have not had much experience measuring feet or meters, provide practice prior to doing this activity.

2. Divide the class into groups of three or four students.

3. Go over the directions for the activity given on the student record sheet.

4. Assist groups with their investigations. (If you can enlist an adult helper for each group, the groups can go around the school to find items to record on their record forms.)

Measuring T-Rex

Name:

1. T-Rex was 50 feet (15 meters) long. Unroll as much string as you think it takes to measure 50 feet (15 meters).

2. Use your measuring stick to cut a piece of string the length of T-Rex. Was your estimate close?   Yes   No

3. Find things around the school that are longer and shorter than T-Rex. Write the names.

These things are longer than T-Rex.	These things are shorter than T-Rex.
_____	_____
_____	_____
_____	_____
_____	_____
_____	_____
_____	_____
_____	_____

A Pteranodon Report

As the label for this pocket states, some prehistoric reptiles took to the air. One of these was *Pteranodon*, a pterosaur of the Late Cretaceous period.

Page 49 provides information about this unusual reptile. You may want to make an overhead transparency to use when sharing the information with your class. Read about *Pteranodon* in library books to see if you can add to the information.

Pages 50 and 51 provide a pattern for a report cover and a drawing of a *Pteranodon* skeleton. Cut writing paper and a construction paper back cover in the same shape.

The booklet can be used to write a report about a *Pteranodon*:

    a. Tell what a *Pteranodon* looked like.
    b. Tell what a *Pteranodon* ate.
    c. Tell how a *Pteranodon* got its food.
    d. Tell how a *Pteranodon* moved.

Or you may wish to have students write a creative story about *Pteranodon*:

    My Ride on a Pteranodon
    Pteranodon Goes Fishing
    If Pteranodon Were Alive Today

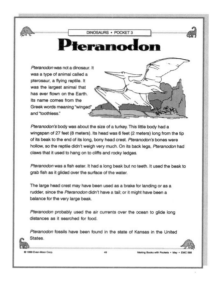

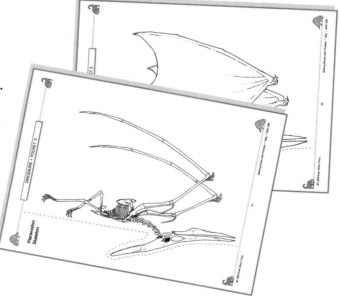

Pteranodon

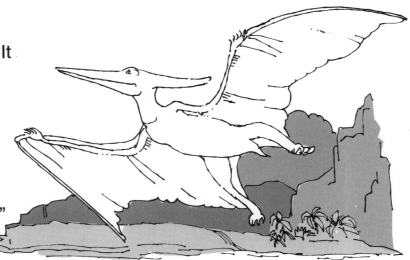

Pteranodon was not a dinosaur. It was a type of animal called a pterosaur, a flying reptile. It was the largest animal that has ever flown on the Earth. Its name comes from the Greek words meaning "winged" and "toothless."

Pteranodon's body was about the size of a turkey. This little body had a wingspan of 27 feet (8 meters). Its head was 6 feet (2 meters) long from the tip of its beak to the end of its long, bony head crest. *Pteranodon's* bones were hollow, so the reptile didn't weigh very much. On its back legs, *Pteranodon* had claws that it used to hang on to cliffs and rocky ledges.

Pteranodon was a fish eater. It had a long beak but no teeth. It used the beak to grab fish as it glided over the surface of the water.

The large head crest may have been used as a brake for landing or as a rudder, since the *Pteranodon* didn't have a tail; or it might have been a balance for the very large beak.

Pteranodon probably used the air currents over the ocean to glide long distances as it searched for food.

Pteranodon fossils have been found in the state of Kansas in the United States.

**Pteranodon
Book Cover**

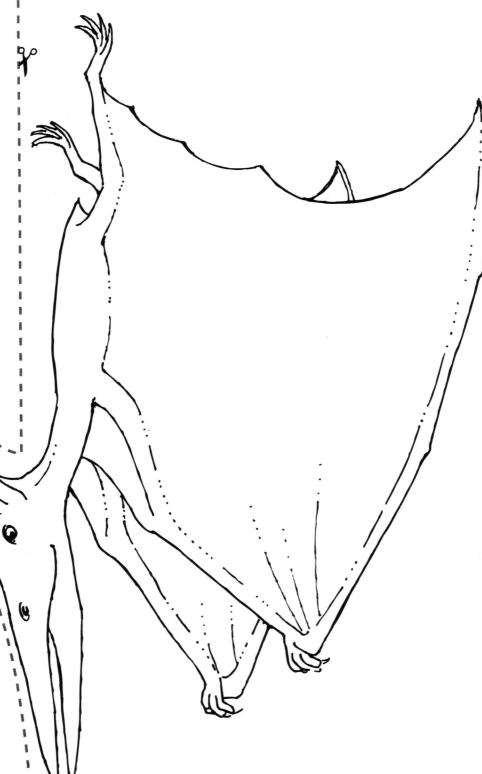

Pteranodon Skeleton

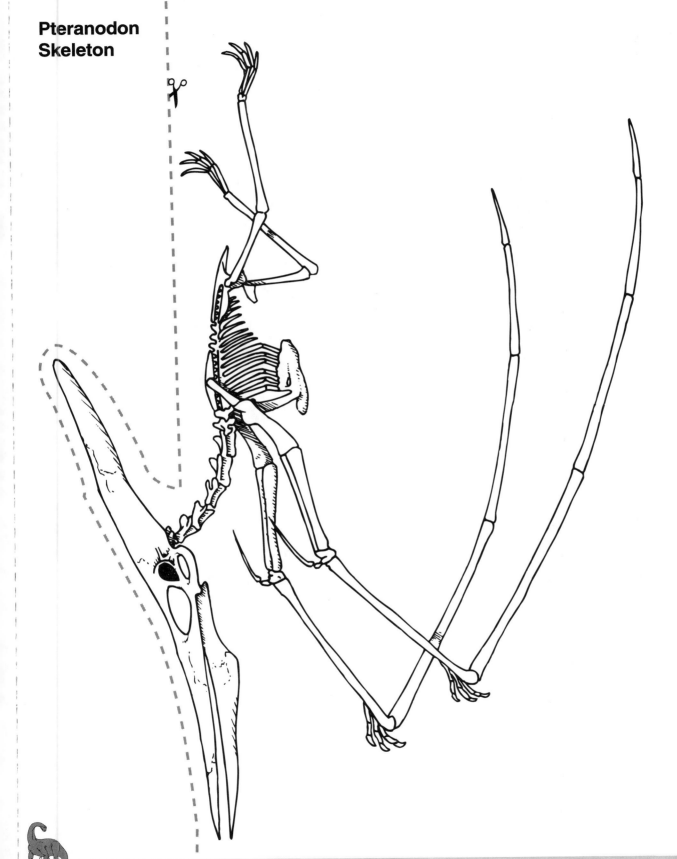

Where Did Dinosaurs Walk?

This book project will help students to understand that dinosaurs lived all over the world.

Materials

- book cover on page 53, reproduced on brown construction paper
- 9" x 12" (23 x 30.5 cm) brown construction paper
- writing form on page 54, reproduced on copier paper—4 per student
- maps and dinosaurs on page 55, reproduced on copier paper
- classroom-size map of the world
- pencil
- scissors
- stapler

Where Did Dinosaurs Walk?

Name: _

Steps to Follow

1. Cut out the book cover. Use it as a template to cut the back cover from the other sheet of brown paper.

2. Cut out the 4 writing forms and staple them between the covers.

3. Cut out the 4 separate maps and dinosaurs and glue one to each writing form.

4. As a class, look at the areas marked for each dinosaur. Locate these areas on the world map and name the location. Write on the chalkboard the name of each dinosaur and its location.

   Spinosaurus—Egypt

   Velociraptor—Asia

   Iguanodon—Europe

   Ankylosaurus—North America

5. Have students write a sentence about where each dinosaur lived. Conclude the book with a summary sentence, such as:

   Dinosaurs lived all over the Earth.

Making Books with Pockets • May • EMC 588

Book Cover

Where Did Dinosaurs Walk?

Name: _____

Writing Form

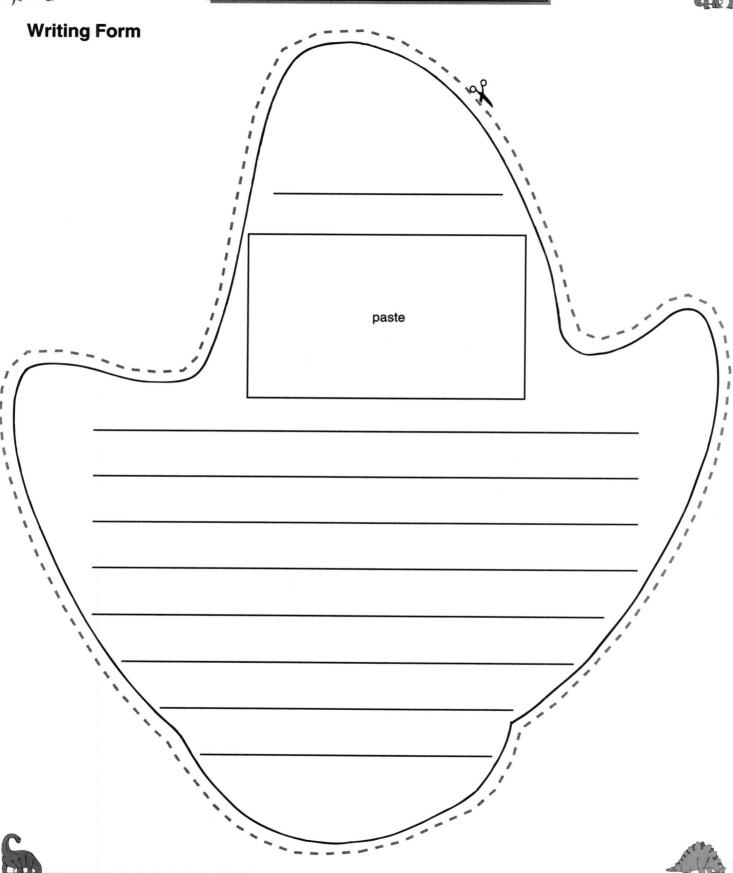

paste

Map Clip Art

Spinosaurus

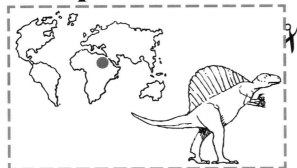

Iguanodon

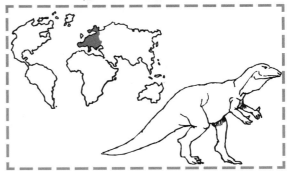

Velociraptor

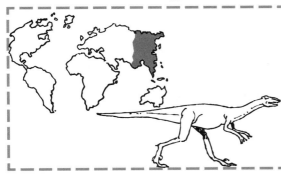

Ankylosaurus

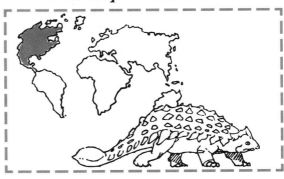

Spinosaurus

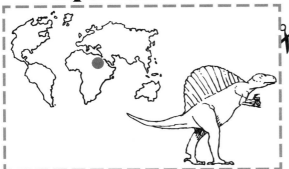

Iguanodon

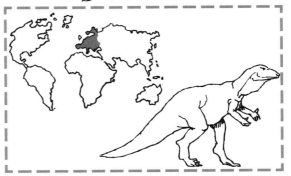

Velociraptor

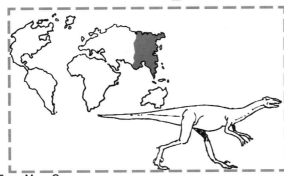

Ankylosaurus

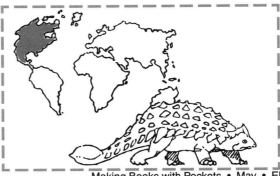

How Did Dinosaurs Become Extinct?

Background

Share current information about theories of dinosaur extinction with your class. Perhaps the most up-to-date information can be found on the World Wide Web. As sites do change, none are given here. However, if you go to Yahooligans.com, Yahoo's search engine for kids, you will see a link to dinosaurs under Science & Oddities on the home page. But don't expect to find definitive information, rather you will find theories that present some very disparate ideas.

Basically, scientists tend to be divided into two camps:

- those that think a single catastrophic event, such as an asteroid or comet impact caused mass extinction of the dinosaurs,

- those that think climatic changes aided by volcanic activity and continental drift caused a gradual demise of these creatures.

Some of the older books that you have in your library may present theories that are now considered invalid by a majority of paleontologists. It's good to point out to students that scientists often have to "throw out" a theory when new information is discovered that shows it to be wrong.

Make a Pop-up Book

Students will make a two-page pop-up book that presents the two most widely held theories mentioned above.

You may want to write the text for each page as a class, having students copy it into their pop-up books. For example:

> The Earth was changing. Continents were moving apart and the warm oceans were shrinking. There were many volcanoes that filled the air with dust, blocking sunlight. Over many years, the climate became cooler, and the dinosaurs gradually died out.

> A giant asteroid or a swarm of comets crashed into the Earth. The huge dust clouds caused by the impact blocked the sunlight. Plants died and the dinosaurs starved to death.

If your students are able, you may want them to generate their own information.

How Did Dinosaurs Become Extinct?

Pop-Up Book

Materials

- book cover design on page 58, reproduced for each student
- 9" x 12" (23 x 30.5 cm) construction paper for cover
- 2 copies of the pop-up pattern on page 59, reproduced on light-colored construction paper
- volcano and asteroid patterns on page 60, reproduced on brown paper
- scraps of red, yellow, and orange construction paper
- scissors
- glue
- crayons

Steps 1 and 2

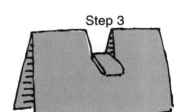

Step 3

Steps to Follow

To make the pop-up forms:

1. Fold each page on the fold line.

2. Cut through both layers on the cut lines.

3. Refold the paper so that the printed side is inside. Fold the tab down and crease it. Fold the tab back up.

4. Open the paper. Pull the tab toward the writing lines until the paper closes. Crease all folds.

Step 4

To add the volcano and asteroid:

1. Cut out the volcano and asteroid patterns.

2. Add "lava" to the volcano using red scraps.

3. Cut strips of red, orange, and yellow and glue them to the asteroid for a fiery effect.

4. Put glue on the pop-up tabs and affix the volcano and the asteroid.

volcano

5. Add a background with crayons. For example, on the asteroid page, color stars, the moon, and the Earth.

asteroid

To put the book together:

1. Close both pop-up pages. Put glue on the back of the side of the volcano that has the writing lines.

2. Lay the background side of the asteroid page on the glue and press.

3. Fold the cover paper in half. Open it up.

4. Lay the folded 2-page pop-up inside the cover. Apply glue to the back of the pop-up page and press the cover closed.

5. Flip the cover over. Open the cover and apply glue to the back of the other pop-up page. Close the cover and press firmly.

6. Color and cut out the book cover design and glue it to the front of the book.

7. Write about the extinction theories represented by the pop-ups on each page. Be sure to end with "But no one really knows what happened to the dinosaurs."

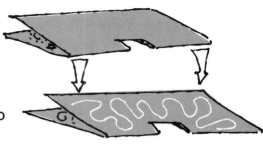

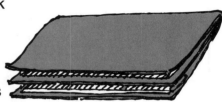

How Did Dinosaurs Become Extinct?

Name

How Did Dinosaurs Become Extinct?

Name

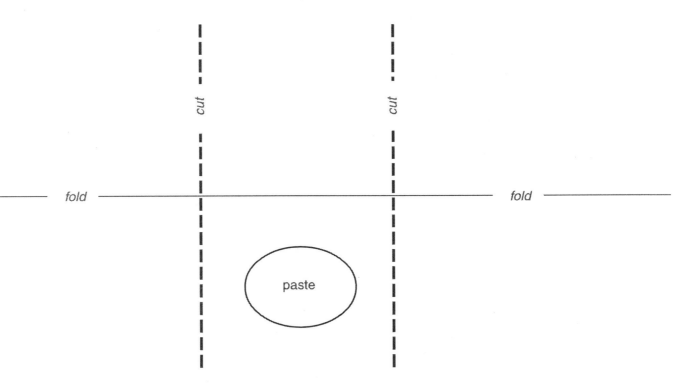

cut

cut

fold

fold

paste

Volcano and Asteroid Patterns

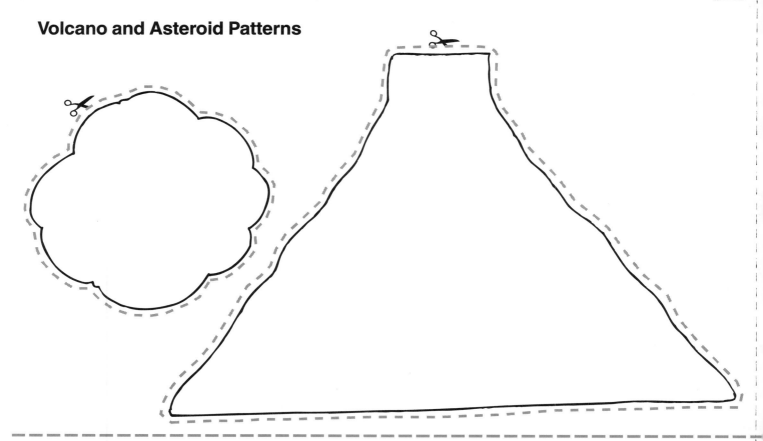

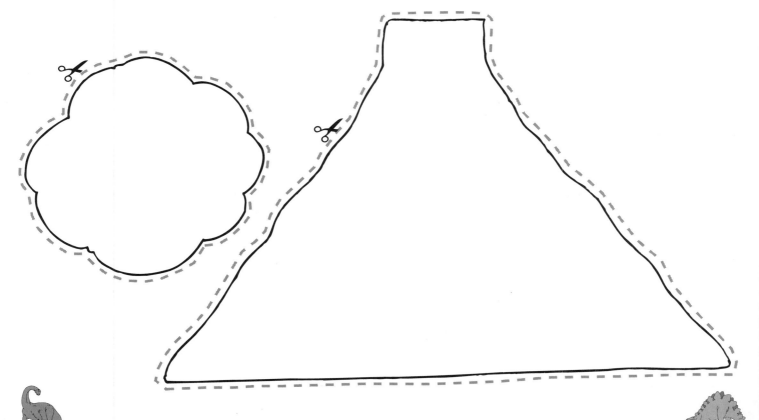

If I Were a Dinosaur

Read *A Dinosaur Named After Me* by Bernard Most (Harcourt Brace & Co., 1991). After hearing the story, students will have the idea of how to make up a dinosaur name that includes their names.

Make an overhead transparency of page 62 and discuss the Greek prefixes and suffixes given. As a class, make up some "dinosaur" names using the names of several students.
For example:

> *CompsoMariasaurus* (pretty Maria lizard)
> *VelociBrianopod* (speedy footed Brian)

Reproduce page 63 for students to create their own dinosaur names and then fill in the blanks to complete the "If I Were a Dinosaur" poem.

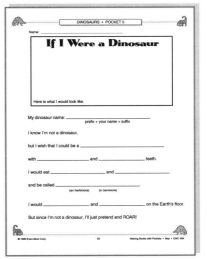

Dinosaur Names

Dinosaur names are taken from Greek words. If you know what some of the Greek words mean, you can learn a lot about each dinosaur from the name alone. For example:

Tyrannosaurus Rex means king of the tyrant lizards.

Greek Prefixes	English Meaning	Greek Suffixes
aqua	water	pod -------- foot
auri	ear	saurus -- lizard
brachio	arm	rex --------- king
di	two	odon ------ tooth
tri	three	
labio	lips	
piro	fire	
naso	nose	
oculo	eye	
dino	terrible	
ptero	wing	
gnathus	jaw	
nychus	claw	
veloci	speedy	
tyrranno	tyrant	
ceros	horn	
compso	pretty	
masso	bulky	
cephalo	head	

Name: _____

If I Were a Dinosaur

Here is what I would look like.

My dinosaur name: _____
prefix + your name + suffix

I know I'm not a dinosaur,

but I wish that I could be a _____

with _____ and _____ teeth.

I would eat _____ and _____

and be called _____.
(an herbivore)   (a carnivore)

I would _____ and _____ on the Earth's floor.

But since I'm not a dinosaur, I'll just pretend and ROAR!

 Making Books with Pockets • May • EMC 588

Note: Reproduce this page and page 65 to label each of the five pockets of the Dinosaurs book.

Some dinosaurs were herbivores.

Pocket 1

Some dinosaurs were carnivores.

Pocket 2

Some prehistoric reptiles could fly.

Pocket 3

Where did dinosaurs live and what happened to them?

Pocket 4

If I were a dinosaur...

Pocket 5

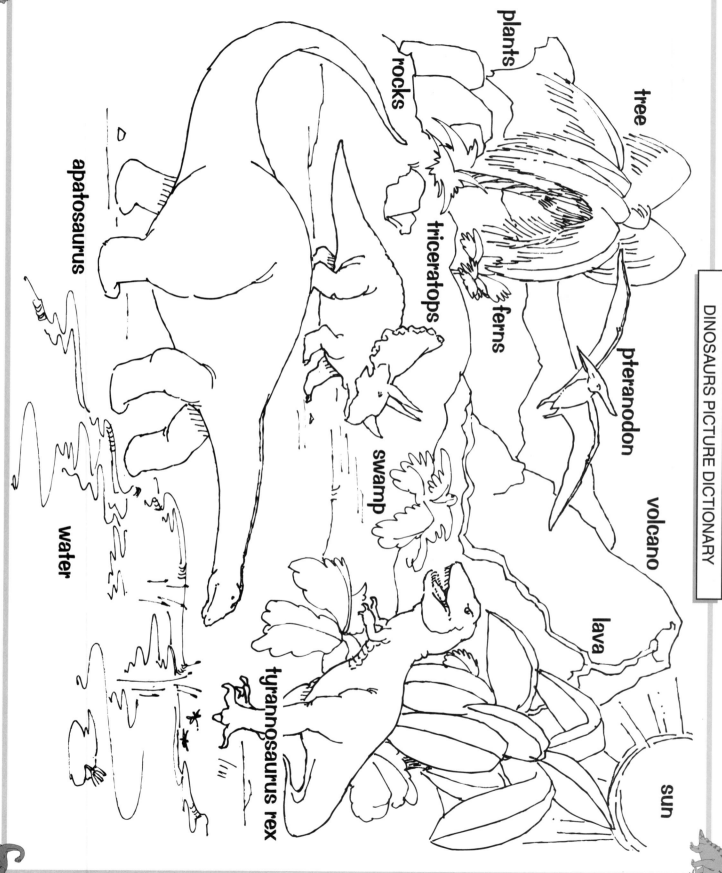

plants

rocks

tree

triceratops

ferns

pteranodon

apatosaurus

swamp

volcano

water

lava

tyrannosaurus rex

sun

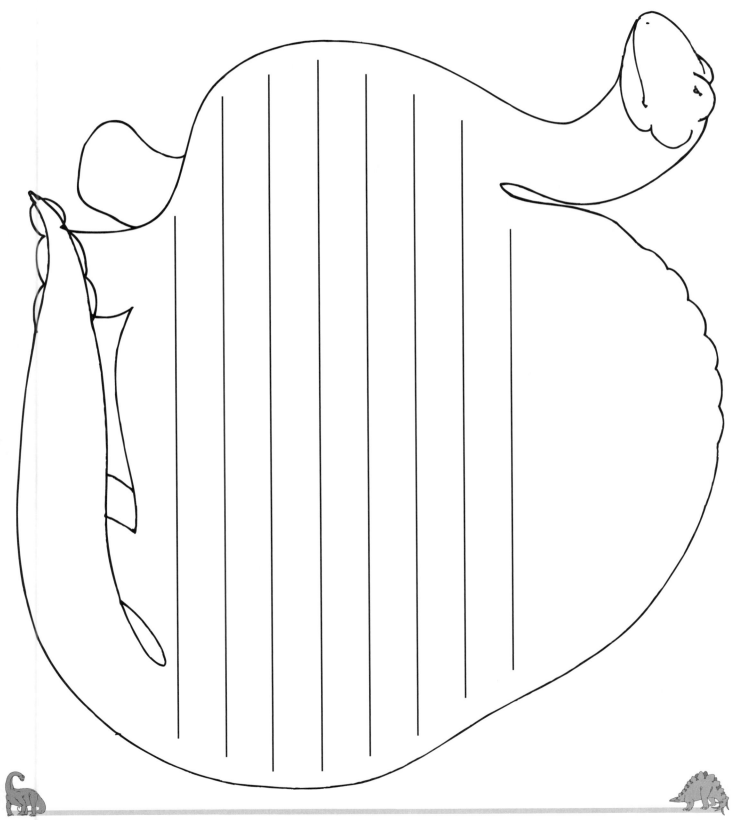

Plants

What better time than May to study plants! This pocket book makes a perfect supplement to a science unit on plants. Students will create charming projects about fruits, vegetables, flowers, and other parts of plants.

BIBLIOGRAPHY

Apple Tree by Barrie Watts; Silver Burdett Press, 1986.
The Carrot Seed by Ruth Krauss; Harper Trophy, 1973.
Eating the Alphabet by Lois Ehlert; Harcourt Brace & Co., 1989.
A Field of Sunflowers by Neil Johnson; Scholastic, 1997.
Flower by Moira Butterfield; Simon & Schuster, 1992.
Flower Garden by Eve Bunting; Harcourt Brace, 1994.
Flowers by Gallimard Jeunesse; Scholastic, 1991.
How Do Things Grow? by Athea; Troll Associates, 1991.
The Magic School Bus Plants Seeds by Joanna Cole; Scholastic, 1995.
The Reason for a Flower by Ruth Heller; Grosset & Dunlap, 1983.
The Seasons of Arnold's Apple Tree by Gail Gibbons; Harcourt Brace, 1984.
The Seed Song by Judy Saksie; Creative Teaching Press, 1994.
The Tiny Seed by Eric Carle; Simon & Schuster, 1987.
Tops and Bottoms by Janet Stevens; Harcourt Brace, 1995.
Vegetables in the Garden by Pascale de Bourgoing & Gallimard Jeunesse; Scholastic, 1989.

POCKET 1

Apple Facts Accordion Book   **page 73**
After learning about apples, students write apple facts in this folding book.

A Stuffed Carrot   **pages 74 and 75**
Read books and get hands-on with carrots and then make a stuffed paper carrot.

**Where Do They Grow—
Above or Below?**   **pages 76–78**
Brainstorm a list of vegetables that grow above or below the ground, then cut and paste pictures to show where various vegetables grow.

POCKET 2

**Learning about
Flowers**   **pages 79 and 80**
Read suggested books about flowers and then create lists of adjectives, nouns, verbs, and phrases to use in writing a "super flower sentence."

Nasturtium Salad   **page 81**
Even if they are reluctant to eat it, your students will think this activity is great fun! It will be even more special if you've grown the nasturtiums in class. Reproduce the recipe for each student's pocket.

**Life Cycle of a
Flowering Plant**   **pages 82 and 83**
Students color, cut, and paste to show the way a flowering plant grows.

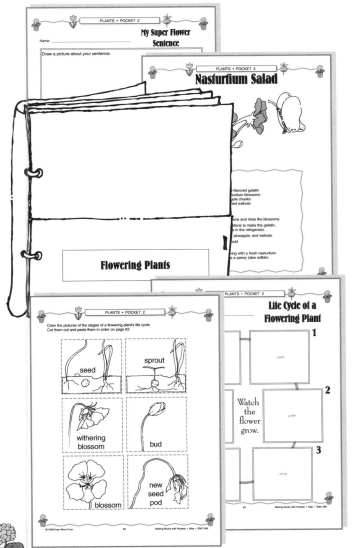

POCKET 3

**Learning about Roots,
Stems, and Leaves**   **page 84**
Hands-on ideas to help your students
discover what these plant parts are like.

**Roots, Stems, and
Leaves Minibook**   **pages 85 and 86**
Read to learn science information about
these plant parts. Students cut apart the
pages and staple them into a four-page
minibook.

Parts of a Plant Flip Book   **pages 87–89**
Flip over the flower, stem, leave, and root
pictures and write about each of these
plant parts.

Parts of a Plant

PLANTS • POCKET 3

Roots, Stems, and Leaves

Name: _____

Materials

- 12" x 18" (30.5 x 45.5 cm) brown construction paper
- labels on page 72
- 1 package of seeds (any kind)
- 1 craft stick or tongue depressor
- scraps of construction paper—all colors
- glue

Teacher Preparation

Carefully slice open the bottom of the seed packets. Remove the seeds and place them in labeled self-lock bags or envelopes for later use.

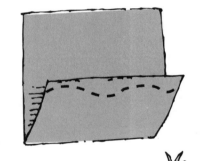

Steps to Follow

1. Fold the brown paper to make a 12" (30.5 cm) square pocket.

2. Cut the folded-up edge in a wave so that it resembles the ground.

3. Let students choose a packet of seeds. Glue the stick to the inside of the seed packet. Glue packet and stick to the cover with the end of the stick inside the pocket.

4. Use construction paper pieces to make plants growing in the ground (carrots, pumpkins, radishes, etc.).

5. Add a sun torn from yellow construction paper.

6. Have students write their names on the "How does _____'s garden grow?" label. Cut out the label and glue it onto the cover.

Use the Seeds
1. Glue several of each kind of seed to an individual paper plate and label the plates. Have students arrange the plates in order from smallest to largest seeds.
2. Plant some seeds in milk cartons or pots and keep a plant log to see which types of seeds sprout first and to record growth rates.

How does _____'s
your name
garden grow?

How does _____'s
your name
garden grow?

How does _____'s
your name
garden grow?

 Making Books with Pockets • May • EMC 588

Apple Facts
Accordion Book

Gather information about apples to prepare for making a book in the shape of an apple:

- Read *The Seasons of Arnold's Apple Tree* by Gail Gibbons and *Apple Tree* by Barrie Watts. Discuss what was learned and write facts to remember on a chart.
- Visit a World Wide Web site called *Cool Stuff about Apples* sponsored by Dole Food Company as a part of their education program. Learn basic information about different varieties of apples—http://www.dole5aday.com/cool-stuff/apple/apple.type.html.
- Conduct an apple tasting and generate a list of words that describe the taste of various apples—tart, crisp, juicy, crunchy, sweet, tangy, etc.

Materials

- 6" x 18" (15 x 45.5 cm) red construction paper
- scraps of brown and green construction paper
- 4" (10 cm) square writing paper—7 per student
- scissors
- glue
- pencil
- black marking pen

Steps to Follow

1. Fold the red paper as shown.

2. Cut the top and bottom edge to make the apple shape.

3. Cut a stem and leaf and glue them to the back side of the front page.

4. Write "Apple Facts" on the cover with a black marking pen.

5. Write one fact about apples on each piece of writing paper.

6. Glue an apple fact to each page of the book.

A Stuffed Carrot

Carrots may be the one vegetable that passes the kid-taste-test— french fries don't count! Explore carrots and then create a stuffed carrot to put in the "Fruits and Vegetables" pocket.

Read *The Carrot Seed* by Ruth Krauss. Give each child some carrot seeds and a whole carrot. Compare the sizes and weights using nonstandard measurement.

- The carrot seed is about the size of (a tiny gnat, a speck of dust, the head of a pin). It grows into a carrot as long as (Adam's foot, my lunchbox, a ruler).
- A carrot seed weighs no more than (a dandelion puff, a grain of sand, a hair). A carrot weighs about as much as (a sandwich, a box of crayons, the chalkboard eraser).

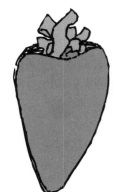

Materials

- two 6" x 12" (15 x 30.5 cm) pieces of orange construction paper
- eight 1" x 6" (2.5 x 15 cm) strips of green tissue paper
- tagboard templates made from the pattern on page 75
- strips of newspaper or plastic bags
- glue

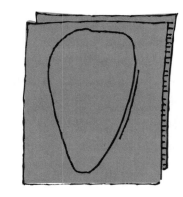

Steps to Follow

1. Trace two orange carrots using the template.

2. Cut or tear out the carrots. (Torn paper gives a more interesting look, but is harder for young students to do.)

3. Glue both carrot pieces together, leaving an opening at the top to stuff. Stuff carrot with newspaper strips or strips of plastic bags.

4. Put tissue paper strips in the top opening of the carrot to represent leaves and glue the carrot closed.

5. "Scrunch" the tissue.

           Making Books with Pockets • May • EMC 588

Carrot Template

Where Do They Grow—Above or Below?

It's interesting for students to discover that lots of the foods we eat grow under the ground.

Before reading *Tops and Bottoms* by Janet Stevens, prepare a chart divided into two sections. Head the sections "Above the Ground" and "Below the Ground." After reading the book, brainstorm a list of vegetables in each category.

Above the Ground	Below the Ground
asparagus	carrots
artichokes	radishes
broccoli	potatoes
cauliflower	beets
peppers	onions
lettuce	garlic
herbs	peanuts
celery	turnips
tomatoes	parsnips

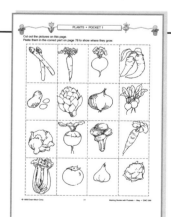

Reproduce pages 77 and 78 for each student. Direct students to cut out the pictures on page 77 and paste them in the correct section of page 78 to show where the food items grow.

Cut out the pictures on this page.
Paste them in the correct part on page 78 to show where they grow.

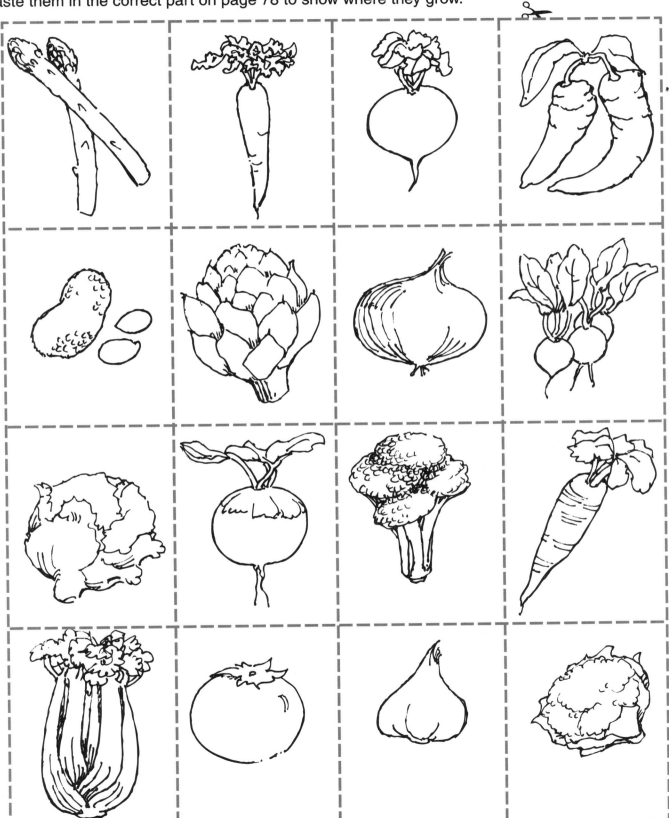

Where Do They Grow?

Above the Ground

paste	paste	paste	paste
paste	paste	paste	paste

Below the Ground

paste	paste	paste	paste
paste	paste	paste	paste

78

Learning about Flowers

Flowers exemplify the saying, "More than just a pretty face." Students may not know that flowers produce the seeds that produce new plants.

Read Eve Bunting's *Flower Garden* and Ruth Heller's *The Reason for a Flower*. Discuss what students learned about flowers. Be sure to point out that vegetables and fruits start out as flowers—that flowers aren't just what we make bouquets from. Brainstorm adjectives, nouns, verbs, and phrases about flowers. List them on a chart divided like the one below.

Flowers

Adjectives (Descriptive Words)	Nouns (Naming Words)	Verbs (Action Words)	Phrases (Where, When, How)
pretty	flower	grew	in my grandma's garden
fragrant	blossom	bloomed	cheerfully on the windowsill
colorful	zinnia	smelled	like sweet perfume
vibrant	daffodil	waved	gently in the spring breeze

Create oral sentences using words and phrases from each section of the chart.
The pretty daffodil bloomed cheerfully on the windowsill.

When students understand the concept of constructing these "super sentences," give each of them a copy of the writing form on page 80 on which to write and illustrate one super sentence. Encourage capable writers to use words and phrases of their own.

My Super Flower Sentence

Name: _____

Draw a picture about your sentence.

_____

_____

_____

_____

_____

_____

Nasturtium Salad

Ingredients

- 1 package of lime-flavored gelatin
- 2 handfuls of nasturtium blossoms
- 1 scoop of pineapple chunks
- ½ scoop of chopped walnuts

Steps to Follow

1. Pick off the flower stems and rinse the blossoms.

2. Follow package directions to make the gelatin, letting it set up a little in the refrigerator.

3. Stir in the blossoms, pineapple, and walnuts.

4. Pour into a pan or mold.

5. Chill until firm.

6. Decorate each serving with a fresh nasturtium blossom—or maybe a pansy (also edible).

Color the pictures of the stages of a flowering plant's life cycle.
Cut them out and paste them in order on page 83.

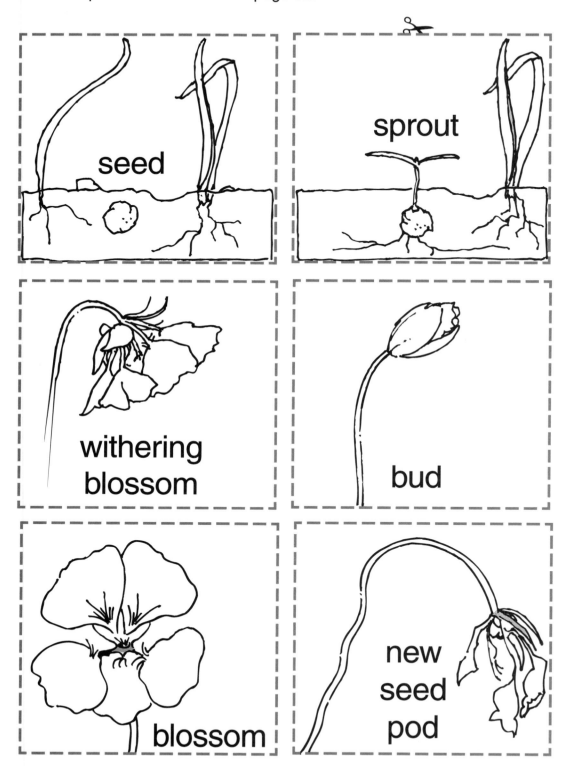

seed

sprout

withering
blossom

bud

blossom

new
seed
pod

Life Cycle of a Flowering Plant

Name: _____

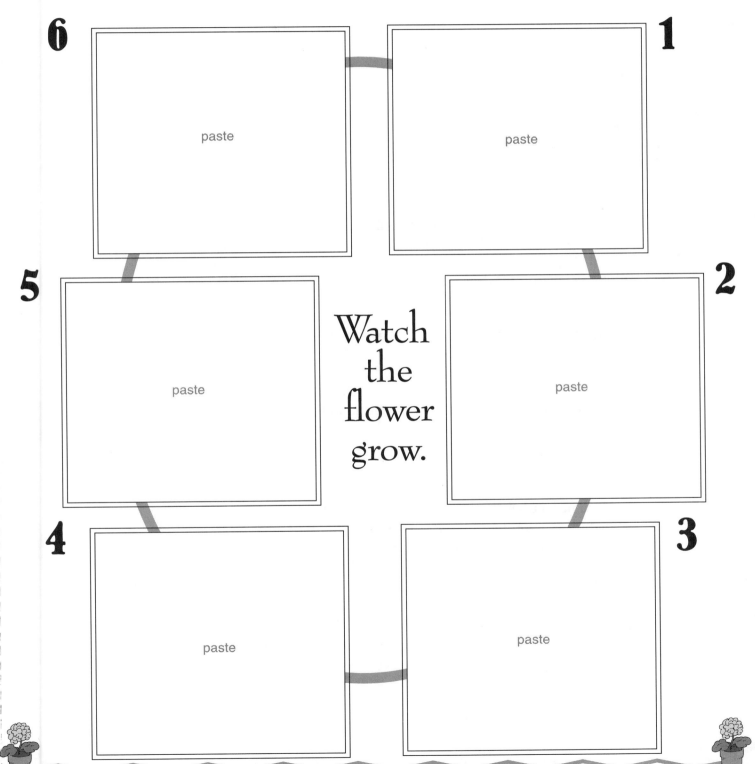

6

paste

1

paste

5

paste

Watch
the
flower
grow.

2

paste

4

paste

3

paste

Making Books with Pockets • May • EMC 588

Learning about
Roots, Stems, and Leaves

Pockets 1 and 2 have provided activities to learn about fruits, vegetables, and flowers. Here are some suggested experiences to familiarize students with other plant parts— roots, stems, and leaves.

Roots, Stems, and Leaves Minibook

Reproduce pages 85 and 86 for each student. Cut the pages apart and staple to make a book. After reading the book together, students may want to color the pictures.

Make a "Root Museum"

• Bring in plants that show variations in root structure:
  a small flowering plant such as a petunia or marigold
  a carrot or turnip with a thick, fleshy root
  a clump of sod with threadlike roots
  an orchid or other plant with aerial roots

• Examine the roots and talk about the differences and similarities. Start a "Root Museum." Ask students to bring in examples of roots to add to the museum. Set out your root display on a long strip of butcher paper. Encourage students to record observations and comparisons directly on the paper.

Examine Stems

• Collect and examine various kinds of stems:
  woody stems such as those on a potted azalea or rose
  soft, fleshy stems such as those found on impatiens or cyclamen
  trailing stems such as those found on pothos or strawberries
• Set up a display similar to the "Root Museum," adding samples that students contribute.

Collect Leaves

• Collect many kinds of leaves. Learn the parts of a leaf—veins, midrib, blade.
• Classify the leaf collection by type—simple, compound, needles.

Roots, Stems, and Leaves

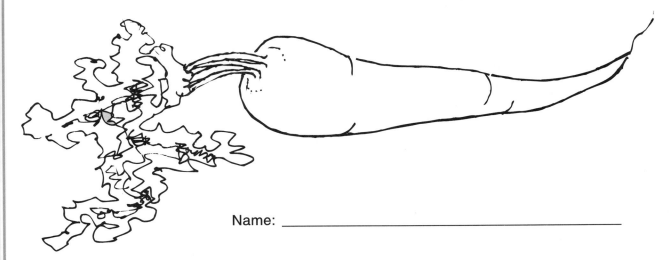

Name: _____

Making Books with Pockets • May • EMC 588

© 1999 Evan-Moor Corp.

Roots

Roots hold a plant in place. Roots take the water and minerals from the soil and carry them to the stem where they are carried to the rest of the plant. Some plants store food in the roots.

Here are some roots people eat.

Making Books with Pockets • May • EMC 588

© 1999 Evan-Moor Corp.

Stems

Stems hold up the leaves and flowers of a plant. Stems have little tubes that carry water and food to the rest of the plant. Grass, flowers, and vines have soft stems. Trees have one hard, wooden stem called a trunk. Most stems grow up toward the sun.

Leaves

A plant can make its own food. The plant uses green cells in the leaves called chlorophyll, water from the soil, carbon dioxide from the air, and energy from sunlight to make food. This is called photosynthesis.

Parts of a
Plant Flip Book

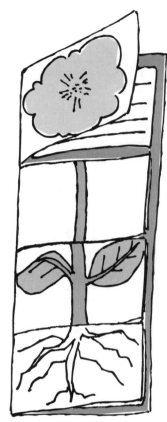

Students will summarize what they have learned about flowers, roots, stems, and leaves to make this flip book.

Materials

- 9" x 12" (23 x 30.5 cm) piece of construction paper
- parts-of-a-plant patterns on page 88
- writing forms on page 89
- crayons
- scissors
- glue

Steps to Follow

1. Fold the construction paper in half lengthwise; then fold it in fourths as shown.

2. Color and cut out the parts of the plant.

3. Glue the plant parts in the correct order on the sections of the construction paper.

4. Cut the picture sections apart on the cut lines.

5. Write about each plant part on the writing forms.

6. Cut out the forms, flip each section of the plant open, and glue each form under its picture.

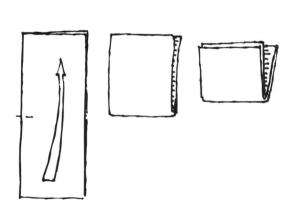

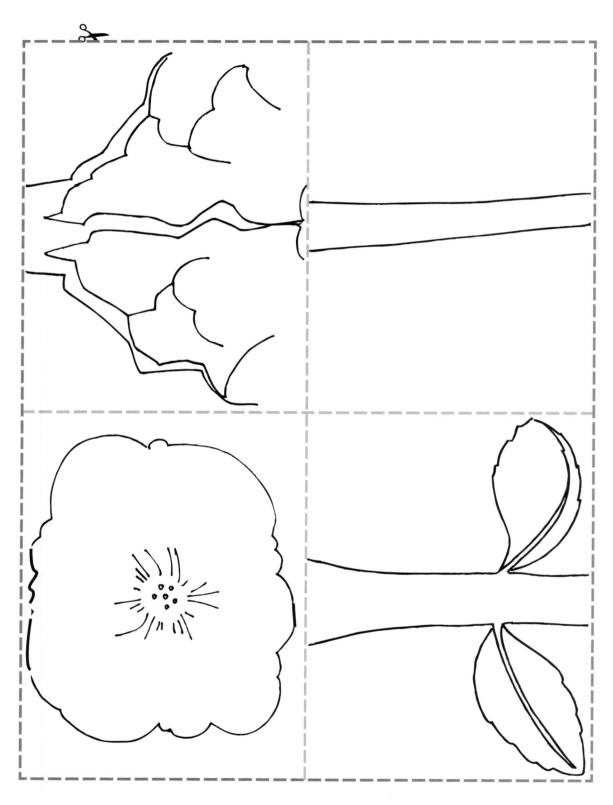

stem

roots

flower

leaves

Note: Reproduce this page to label each of the three pockets of the Plants book.

✂

✂

✂

Fruits and Vegetables

Flowering Plants

Parts of a Plant

Pocket 1

Pocket 2

Pocket 3

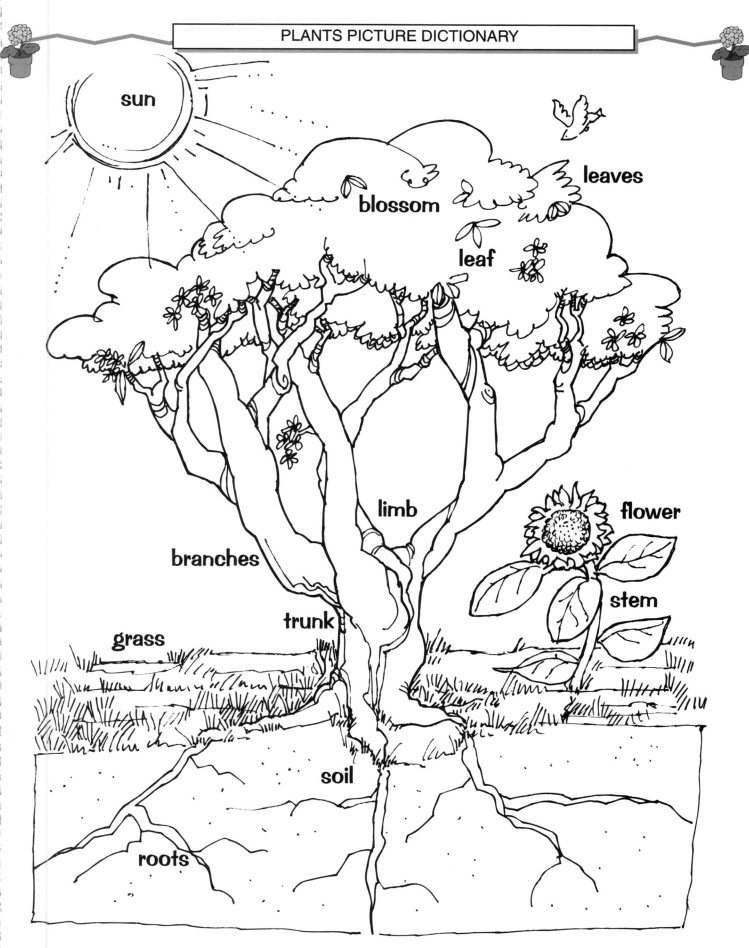

Name: _____

Bulletin Board Bonanza

How Long Was Oviraptor?—page 94

What fun students will have helping to create a life-size dinosaur and then using some unusual measuring instruments to see how long it was!

Materials

- dinosaur pictures
- overhead projector and transparency
- butcher paper
- marking pen
- scissors
- tempera paint and sponges (optional)
- adding machine tape
- nonstandard measuring tools, for example:

straws	toothpicks
crayons	pencils
paper clips	playing cards

A Pumpkin Grows—page 95

This bulletin board changes as the pumpkin goes from a sprout to a huge orange squash.

Materials

- patterns for leaf, sprout, and blossom on page 96
- 1" (2.5 cm) strips of green construction paper or butcher paper for stems
- green and orange construction paper for pumpkins
- brown and blue butcher paper for bulletin board background
- crayons
- scissors

A Bulletin Board of Nonstandard Measurement

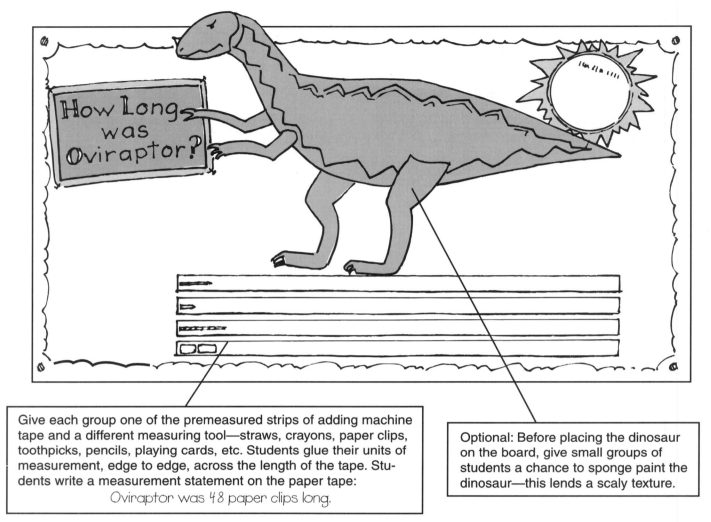

Give each group one of the premeasured strips of adding machine tape and a different measuring tool—straws, crayons, paper clips, toothpicks, pencils, playing cards, etc. Students glue their units of measurement, edge to edge, across the length of the tape. Students write a measurement statement on the paper tape:

Oviraptor was 48 paper clips long.

Optional: Before placing the dinosaur on the board, give small groups of students a chance to sponge paint the dinosaur—this lends a scaly texture.

Before this bulletin board goes up, students will measure the dinosaur using a variety of nonstandard measuring instruments.

Teacher Preparation

1. Choose a dinosaur whose length is appropriate for your bulletin board space. Here are some examples:

> *Oviraptor*–5 feet (2 meters)
> *Stegosaurus*–25 feet (7 meters)
> *Dimetrodon*–10 feet (3 meters)
> *Protoceratops*–6 feet (2 meters)

2. Trace the dinosaur onto an overhead transparency. Then enlarge it by projecting the picture onto a piece of butcher paper cut to the correct length. Move the projector forward or backward until the image reaches the paper length. Trace the outline of the dinosaur onto the butcher paper with a black marker.

Note: If you choose a larger dinosaur, you may have to move to the multipurpose room to do your drawing.

3. Cut strips of adding machine tape to match the length of the dinosaur.

A Bulletin Board That Changes

At first there is just a pumpkin sprout.

Then you add the vine and leaves. Every few days add new leaves and vines.

Next add some yellow blossoms.

Now you pin up small green pumpkins.

The pumpkins grow into larger orange ones.

When the pumpkins are "ripe," you can pick them. Serve pumpkin pie the next day.

Preparing the Bulletin Board

1. Staple the background to the bulletin board as shown and add the caption.
2. Color and cut out the sprout, blossom, and a number of leaves.
3. Cut two sizes of green pumpkins and a number of orange pumpkins of increasing size.
4. Cut a number of green vines of varying lengths.

Patterns for Pumpkin Bulletin Board

Making Books with Pockets • May • EMC 588